SPHYNX CAT
BUTT

ADULT
COLORING BOOK

COLOR TEST PAGE

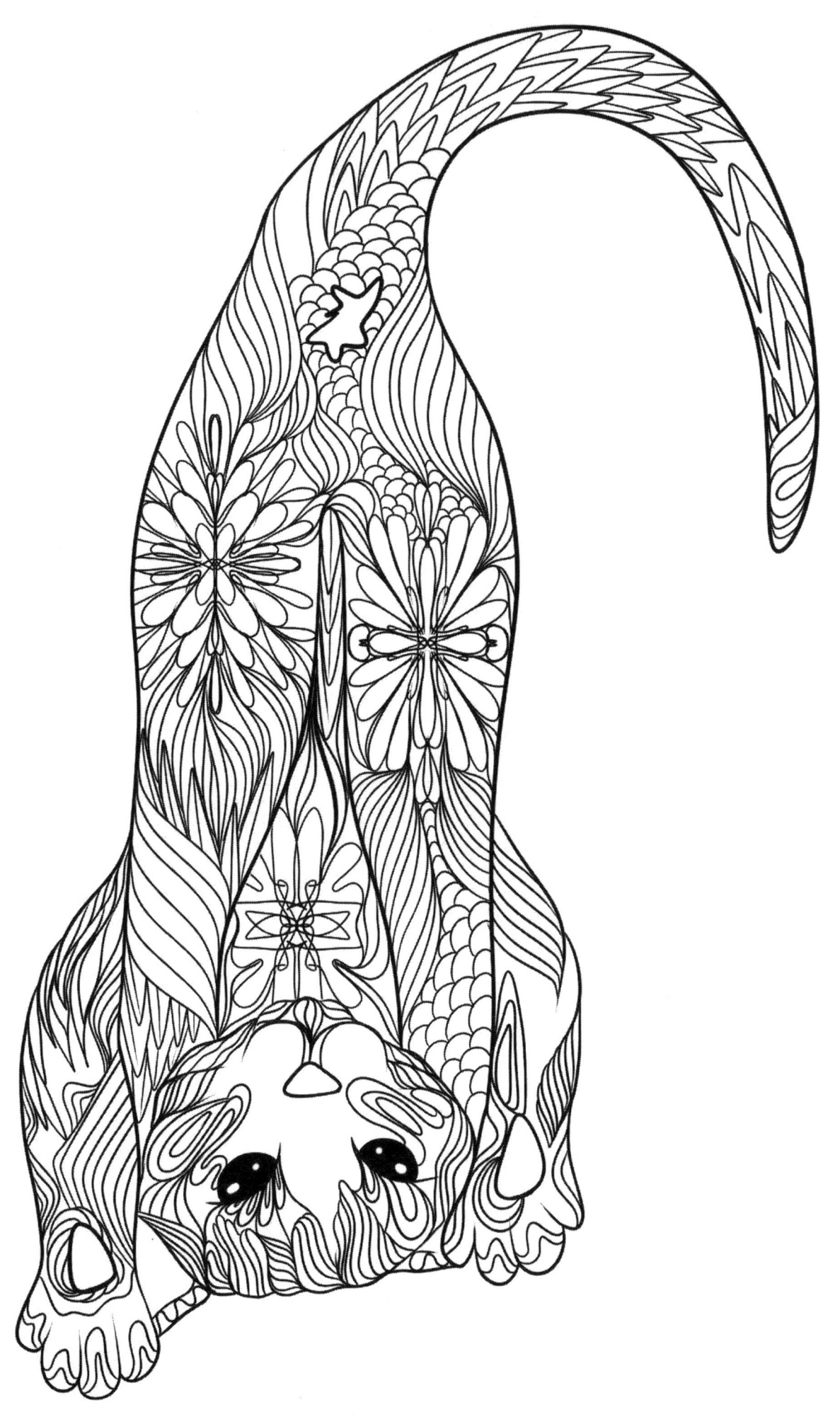

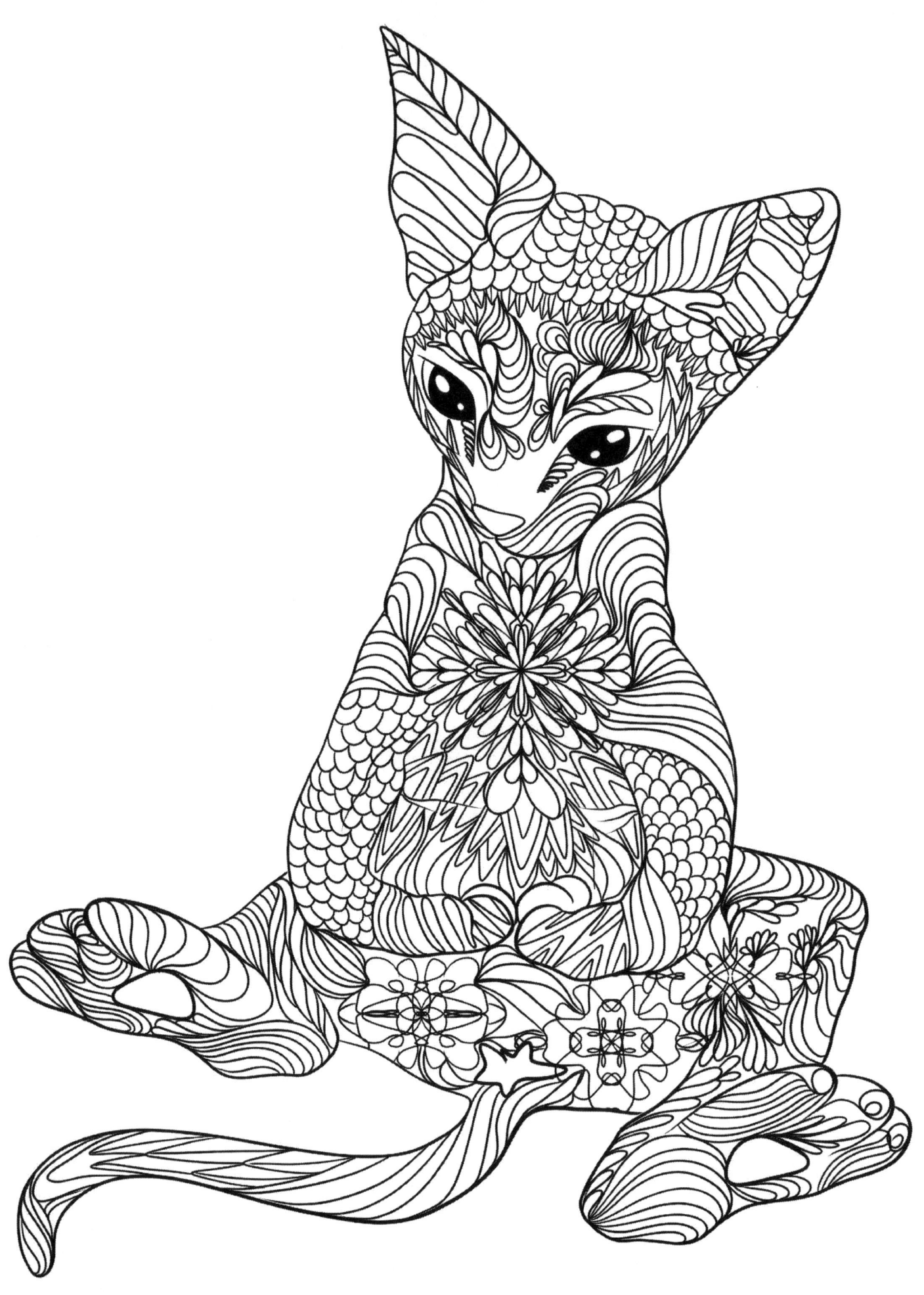

IF YOU LIKED THIS
COLORING BOOK
CONSIDER LEAVING A
REVIEW ON AMAZON

ALSO IF YOU ARE
INTERESTED IN MORE
FUNNY COLORING BOOKS
FOR ADULTS
BE SURE TO CHECK OUT:
,,SILLY GROWN PRESS"
ON AMAZON

Manufactured by Amazon.ca
Bolton, ON

21529142R00031